The Connection Between Your Faith and Thinking

Roy Hayes

The Connection Between Your Faith and Thinking

First Edition: 2022

ISBN: 9781524318123
ISBN eBook: 9781524328153

This book is dedicated to my lovely wife Brenna Hayes who is a strong support in my life.

Table of Contents

"Do something today that your future self will thank you for."

Sean Patrick Flanery

Introduction

It is frustrating and debilitating when you're trying to be all that God has called you to be, but something in your life is weighing you down. It seems to always be holding you back, and it shows up when you least expect it and sabotages your dreams. Moreover, you have no idea what the problem is, and you don't have a clue how solve it.

Well, that was me at one time. That is, until God revealed to me what my problem was and what it would take to outgrow that problem.

Did you hear that? I could *outgrow* my problem. You see, God has created us in a manner where we are supposed to—and can—outgrow our problems by renewing our minds in the Word of God. Because of this understanding, I have been able to overcome some hurdles in my life that I thought I would never clear. Nevertheless, we are all a work in progress, and every day we are to work out our own salvation with the Lord's help.

In this book, my prayer is that I can show the saints of God what their problem is, how to recognize that problem, and how to fix it. I believe that once you get the revelation of this one problem that all Christians have, it will revolutionize every area of your life. As a matter a fact, this one area controls and sets the course for your whole life. So, it's worth the effort to get it fixed.

How to get the most out of this Book

When anyone hears the word of the kingdom, and does not understand it, then the wicked one comes and snatches away what was sown in his heart. This is he who received seed by the wayside.

Matthew 13:19

When you don't understand something, you lose interest in it and eventually forget it. If you forget the Word, then you can't *do* the Word, which, according to James 1:25, is rather important: "But he who looks into the perfect law of liberty and continues in it and is not a forgetful hearer but a doer of the work, this one will be blessed in what he does."

Only those who continue in the Word and are doers of the Word receive the blessings.

Second Timothy 2:7 says, "Consider what I say, and may the Lord give you understanding in all things."

In other words, *think*. Imagine yourself doing the Word and receiving the promise, and the Lord will grant you full insight and understanding in everything.

One sure way of gaining the understanding of what you are reading or listening to is to study it enough until you can teach it yourself. If you can't teach what you have read or heard, you don't understand it yet. Remember, the amount of time and effort you give to the Word will be the same measure you get out of it.

Some questions answered in this book:

- Should I be looking for more faith?
- Do I need to develop my faith?
- Does my faith grow?
- Do I have weak faith?
- How do I get more out of my faith?
- What determines the capacity at which my faith will work?
- Why can't I go further in life?

- Why can't I receive more, do more, or experience more of God's blessings?
- Why can't I get healed?
- What is causing my sickness?
- Why do I fall short in some areas of my life?
- Is faith alone enough for me to receive the promises of God?
- How do I alienate myself from the promises?
- What is the one problem that affects every aspect of my life?
- How do I gain more control of my life?
- How do I experience more peace in my life?

Faith is Never the Problem

Invariably, when Christians encounter problems and don't know how to fix them, they immediately think their faith is the problem. They think, "I need more faith. I need to look for more faith." Or they pray and ask God to increase their faith.

If you don't know what your problem is and don't know how to fix it, then the problem has power and ascendency over you. However, if you know what the problem is, and you know how to fix it, then *you* have the power and ascendency.

Faith is never the problem. Just like wet comes with water, faith comes with being a Christian. When you heard the gospel of Jesus Christ, faith came as a gift from God, which enabled you to give your life to the Lord. That faith created the greatest miracle you will ever receive in this lifetime.

So, faith came. Let that soak in.

Living by Faith is not Optional for a Christian

But without faith it is impossible to please Him, for he who comes to God must believe that He is, and that He is a rewarder of those who diligently seek Him.

Hebrews 11:6

The writer of Hebrews says that to please God, we must believe in the Lord, even though we cannot see Him. In other words, living by faith is not optional for a Christian if he or she is going to live victoriously on the earth. Romans 1:17 says, "The just shall live by faith."

Faith makes everything available for us to be world overcomers because we benefit from what Christ has already done for us. Galatians 4:7 tells us that we are sons of God, and if we are children of God, then we are also His heirs. That means everything Christ has done and has accomplished belongs to us! Faith in Christ is what makes this a reality in our lives. Romans 5:2 says that through Him, "we have access by faith into this grace in which we stand."

Continue to grow in faith, and daily examine yourself to make sure you understand how to walk and live by this law of faith. (See Rom. 3:27.)

We Have Faith

God hath dealt to every man the measure of faith.

Romans 12:3 KJV

Everybody has natural faith. We are guided by our senses—what we can see or feel. But those of us who are born again have supernatural faith, where we believe even when we have no evidence from our five physical senses. This is a supernatural faith from God. And Paul is addressing people who have placed their faith and trust in Jesus Christ.

I am crucified with Christ: nevertheless, I live; yet not I, but Christ liveth in me: and the life which I now live in the flesh I live by the faith of the Son of God, who loved me, and gave himself for me.

Galatians 2:20 KJV

You see, it is not our faith that we are living by. The faith that is in our born-again spirit is the faith of Jesus. It is this same faith that gave Peter the ability to walk on water. In the natural it is impossible to walk on water, but with faith, all things are possible. Peter himself says that we who are born-again "have obtained like precious faith"—that same water-walking faith that he had (2 Pet. 1:1).

It did not say you need to look for more faith or pray for more faith. You have already obtained world-overcoming faith!

So, we know now that we have the faith of Jesus in our born-again spirit. It's a faith that is limitless and all-powerful. It never fails or faulters or becomes weak in any way because, after all, it is the faith of Jesus.

For assuredly, I say to you, if you have faith as a mustard seed, you will say to this mountain, "Move from here to there," and it will move; and nothing will be impossible for you.

Matthew 17:20

Jesus is saying, you won't need any more than mustard seed sized faith to overcome any problem you encounter in your lifetime. Mustard seed sized faith will annihilate any sickness, any disease, any poverty or lack, and any adversity or opposition while you are living here on the earth.

Mustard seed size faith puts you in the realm where all things are possible.

Yet you have much more faith than that mustard seed because it took *great* faith for you to become a new creature in Christ Jesus.

Has Faith Come or
is it Coming?

So then faith comes by hearing, and hearing by the word of God.

Romans 10:17

This Scripture can cause problems in the life of a Christian if it is taken out of context. If you don't read to find out what the whole thought is, you might think that you have to keep reading—or hearing—the Word to get more faith. However, we have uncovered a number of Scriptures that say otherwise.

I used to think that if I just kept hearing the Word, I would get more faith. Simple. But that kept me on a quest of always looking for more faith. So, when I encountered a problem, I thought I needed more Word so I could get more faith. It was never-ending. Yet I already had all the faith I needed to solve my problem.

You see, all I needed was faith the size of a mustard seed, but I already had much more faith than that. The problem was, I was not able to use that faith because I didn't realize that I had it or that I had *enough*. This idea that "faith comes by hearing," when read out of context, caused me to always be looking for more faith, and because I was always looking for more, it meant that I wasn't relying on the faith I already had.

If you notice, the context of this verse is talking about faith for salvation. So, when you heard the gospel of Jesus Christ, God gifted you with faith, and you received salvation (see Eph. 2:8). That faith was the faith of Jesus, and it was powerful enough to create the greatest miracle you will ever experience in your lifetime.

Now let's look at that verse in context.

If you confess with your mouth the Lord Jesus and believe in your heart that God has raised Him from the dead, you will be saved. For with the heart one believes unto righteousness, and with the mouth confession is made unto salvation. For the Scripture says, "Whoever believes on Him will not be put to shame." For there is no distinction between

Jew and Greek, for the same Lord over all is rich to all who call upon Him. For "whoever calls on the name of the Lord shall be saved."

How then shall they call on Him in whom they have not believed? And how shall they believe in Him of whom they have not heard? And how shall they hear without a preacher? . . .

So then faith comes by hearing, and hearing by the word of God.

Romans 10:9–14, 17

So, does that mean we don't need to keep hearing and reading the Word of God if faith has already come? Of course not. The more you see and hope for what is revealed to you in the Word, the more substance your faith will create for you.

You see, after you have received faith, you will need revelation knowledge. Revelation knowledge is when you have not been able to "see" something, but now you're able to see it. You "see" a divine image from the Word. The Bible calls that "hope." Without hope—that divine image of what belongs to you in Christ—faith has nothing to create substance in your life.

Hebrews 11:1 says, "Now faith is the substance of things hoped for, the evidence of things not seen." You've heard it said that faith begins where the will of God is known. Well, this where that statement comes from. And hope is what gives faith its assignment to create substance in your life.

Once the will of God is revealed to you by giving you hope, painting a picture in your heart, and showing you what you have, who you are, and what you can do in Christ Jesus, then the faith you already have in your born-again spirit can create that substance in your life.

Simon Peter, a bondservant and apostle of Jesus Christ, to those who have obtained like precious faith with us by the righteousness of our God and Savior Jesus Christ: Grace and peace be multiplied to you in the knowledge of God and of Jesus our Lord, as His divine power has given to us all things that pertain to life and godliness, through the knowledge of Him who called us by glory and virtue,

2 Peter 1:1–3

Here, the apostle Peter is saying that you're going to get all your needs met in your physical life, and you will get everything you need to grow spiritually as you access the word of His grace through faith.

We have access by faith into this grace in which we stand and rejoice in hope of the glory of God.

Romans 5:2

So now, brethren, I commend you to God and to the word of His grace, which is able to build you up and give you an inheritance among all those who are sanctified.

Acts 20:32

According to Hebrews 4:2, as you mix the Word (the knowledge of God that produces hope) with faith, it will profit you.

The more you hope for, and the more you see what is revealed in the Word to you, the more substance your faith will create for you.

Here is a good saying to keep in mind: Hope writes the check, and faith cashes it.

Finding Your Problem

If faith—or a lack of faith—is not your problem, then what is? And more importantly, how do you fix it?

> My son, give attention to my words; incline your ear to my sayings. Do not let them depart from your eyes; keep them in the midst of your heart; for they are life to those who find them, and health to all their flesh. Keep your heart with all diligence, for out of it spring the issues of life.
>
> Proverbs 4:20–23

The "heart" mentioned here is comprised of your spirit and your soul. We are not talking about your spirit man, the real you. That person was sealed by the Holy Spirit when you got saved (see Eph. 1:13). He or she is perfect, can't sin, and is identical to Jesus. We are talking about your soul, which is your mind, will, and emotions. This passage is talking about your thinking. So, let's exchange "heart" with "thinking" to get a better sense of the deeper meaning:

> Keep your heart [thinking] with all diligence, for out of it spring the issues of life.

> Proverbs 4:23

Your actions are a direct result of the way you think. In other words, you can't act differently than the way you think or see yourself. Your life goes the way you think. Your actions will always reflect your habitual thoughts. Your decisions and actions are fostered and governed by the way you think. Proverbs 23:7 says that you are going to *be* as you *think*. Another way to look at it is that your thinking creates your character and your personality.

The issues you face are neither good nor bad. They are just circumstances. They are just there. However, the reason particular circumstances or issues are in *your* life is because of the way you think or the way you see life.

The issues you may face are sickness or health, poverty or wealth, fear or peace, hatred or love, disharmony in your marriage or harmony, failure or success, etc. These conditions do not come from your spouse, your boss, your president, your parents. No, they are all generated by your thinking.

Guard your heart above all else, for it determines the course of your life.

Proverbs 4:23 NLT

This is saying that if you're not happy with the way your life is going, with 'the course of your life', it is because of your thinking: the pictures you are dwelling on daily, the thoughts you're focusing on, or the imaginations you're conjuring up in your mind.

Your thinking will determine the outcome of your life, ministry, or your church!

How many times have you heard, 'the battle is either won or lost in your mind'? What this means is that you must make controlling your thinking a priority in your life because this is where your life will come from.

Your heart, or thinking, controls your life. It governs your life and tells you how far you will go in life. If you are stuck at a certain level of success, and you can't seem to go any farther in your endeavors, then you may need new thoughts to break the threshold of new accomplishments. Think about it. The thoughts you've had up until now have brought you to your current place in life. This is proof that thoughts determine your course. But to go further, you will need *new* thoughts, a *new* way of thinking. New thoughts equals a new place.

Your thinking sets the conditions of your life and creates your reality. Your heart or the way you think will determine if you are poor or wealthy, sickly or healthy. It will determine if you are a failure or a success in life.

Setting the Prosperity Level of Your Future

You will prosper to the degree or level that your mind is set at. Therefore, you are responsible for where you set the level of your own prosperity.

> Beloved, I pray that you may prosper in all things and be in health, just as your soul prospers.
>
> 3 John verse 2

The difference between a poor man and a wealthy man is way he thinks. You could also say the difference between a sickly person and a healthy person is the way he or she thinks too. Based on Proverbs 4:23, these are issues that come from your heart or from the way you think.

Now, did you notice, 3 John verse 2 does not mention anything about faith? That is because John is addressing Christians who have the faith of Jesus in their born-again spirits.

You see, there is a connection between faith and your thinking. Your thinking will cause your faith to soar to new heights or it will limit its potential in your life.

What is the Connection Between Your Thinking and Your Faith?

Remember the question we discussed earlier: Why do we need to keep reading the Word of God if faith has already come? As you keep reading, it will be made clear to you. So, let's dig a little deeper in the Word.

> Now faith is the substance of things hoped for, the evidence of things not seen.
>
> Hebrews 11:1

God designed faith to create substance out of the things we hope for. Or you could say that your thoughts, imaginations, vision, or the treasure in your heart (which becomes your hope), along with the law of faith will create substance every time you work it because it is a law.

> A good person produces good things from the treasury of a good heart, and an evil person

produces evil things from the treasury of an evil heart.

Matthew 12:35 NLT

Your treasure, or "treasury," is your hope. The treasury of a good heart is your good thoughts, and the treasury of the evil heart is evil thoughts.

The whole of a man's being flows from the deposits in his heart, or the way he thinks. It is what he has stored up with which he makes all his decisions in life.

Hope is the Blueprint
of Your Life

If you want to build your dream home, first you need to come up with a blueprint. Then you're going to have to hire a contractor to build the home to the specifications on your blueprint.

Your blueprint is your hope, and the contractor is your faith. Just like a reputable and proven contractor, faith will build your dream home exactly to your specifications because he is guided by the blueprint you give him. When your home is completed, and if some reason you're not satisfied with the finished product, you can't get upset with the contractor because he built your dream home according to the specs on the blueprint you drew up.

Jesus said, "According to your faith be it unto you" (Matt. 9:29 KJV). In other words, whatever hope, thoughts, visions, or imaginations you give to your faith, it is all faith has to work with to create substance in your life.

You draw up the plans—or the blueprint—for your life by your thoughts, imaginations, hope (the treasure in your heart, whether good or bad). And your contractor will build it for you.

So, you see, your faith is never your problem. It is your heart, or it is the way you think. It is the problem, but it is also the solution.

The law of faith (see Rom. 3:27) is always at work in your life, for your benefit or for your detriment, because faith is always receiving your blueprint. We are told to guard our hearts because faith creates the issues in our lives.

To make the connection between faith and our thinking even clearer, I want to share another example.

Your Thinking Sets the Thermostat for Your Life's Environment

Most of us are familiar with our home's air conditioning unit. It consists of the thermostat and the power unit, or compressor. You set the environment in your home by setting the temperature on the thermostat, which sends a signal to the power unit to deliver the temperature at which you set the thermostat. That power unit will deliver every time because it was designed by the manufacturer to operate that way. But you are the one in charge of setting the thermostat. If you want heat, you set it on heat; if you want cool, you set it on cool.

How does this relate to what we're talking about here? Well, for your life, your hope is the thermostat, and faith is the power unit. Remember, your hope is your thinking, your vision, mindset, and imagination. Whatever you set your thinking (your hope) on, your faith will work until the change is delivered in your life, as long as you leave your hope there.

You must hope, and then wait until your environment is changed. Your faith will create substance out of your hope because the Creator designed it to do just that.

If you don't like the temperature in your home, you set the temperature to your desire: hot or cold. If you don't like the "temperature" of your life, then reset the thermostat. You choose the course of your life by the things you think or meditate on. What occupies your mind is what you give your attention to.

You are choosing your life by the things you think on. Therefore, you must choose thoughts that are beneficial to your success. Whatever you deposit in your heart is going to reveal itself to the world.

Does My Faith Need to be Developed?

Your thinking limits the potential of your faith.

Some people think the faith in their born-again spirit needs to be developed. Thinking this way creates doubt because they're not convinced that their faith will get the job done. The thought is always there that may be if they just developed their faith more, they could deal with their situations better. But this is dangerous thinking, and the devil will always take advantage where he can.

The faith of Jesus that's in your born-again spirit never needs to be developed. Just think, the faith you received when you heard the gospel and received Jesus as your Lord and Savior was powerful and developed enough to create the greatest miracle of your life.

Can you see how weird it sounds when someone says that our faith needs to be developed?

We are the ones who need to be developed, not our faith.

But we can be strong in faith, or we can be weak in faith. Let me give you an example.

If I challenged a trained and developed Olympic swimmer to a race to the end of a pool, I'm going to lose. He has trained and developed himself in the water, and I have not. So, when we are in the water, I am a weak swimmer, and he is a strong swimmer. Notice, the water does not change at all. It is still wet and has all the other characteristics that water has.

Faith never changes. It is always all-powerful and limitless, and it never weakens or faulters. You see, one person can be weak in faith, and another can be strong in faith. But how they operate in faith depends on their development in it.

What is the development I am talking about? It is the development of your thinking; it is having a renewed mind. If you're weak minded, you will never be strong in the Lord and in the power of His might.

How to be Strong in Faith

Your faith will be as strong as your thinking will allow it to be.

Therefore it is of faith that it might be according to grace, so that the promise might be sure to all the seed, not only to those who are of the law, but also to those who are of the faith of Abraham, who is the father of us all (as it is written, "I have made you a father of many nations") in the presence of Him whom he believed—God, who gives life to the dead and calls those things which do not exist as though they did; who, contrary to hope, in hope believed, so that he became the father of many nations, according to what was spoken, "So shall your descendants be." And not being weak in faith, he did not consider his own body, already dead (since he was about a hundred years old), and the deadness of Sarah's womb. He did not waver at the promise of God through unbelief, but was strengthened in faith, giving glory to God, and being fully convinced that what He had promised He was also able to perform. And therefore "it was accounted to him for righteousness."

Romans 4:16–22

Abraham was not weak in faith. He was strong in faith because he believed in the "hope," the picture he had in in his heart. Remember, your hope is your thinking, vision, or your imagination. God's word painted a picture in the heart of Abraham. Even though, in the natural, there was no hope that the promise would come to pass, the image in his heart gave him hope, which strengthened him in faith.

This passage says Abraham wasn't weak in faith because of the things he chose to consider, or rather, "did not consider." The Bible never says that Abraham did not have faith. It makes it clear that he was *in* the faith, and then it stresses that he was not weak *in* it.

Remember, I said, you can have faith, but you can be weak or strong in it because of your thinking, the things you consider. Abraham was strengthened in faith because of the hope in his heart, which was the promise that he would have a son in his and Sarah's old age.

God also gave Abraham something to focus on, something to stimulate his imagination. He gave him a hope to keep him anchored and on course to his future.

God said in Genesis 22:17, "Blessing I will bless you, and multiplying I will multiply your descendants as the stars of the heaven and as the sand which is on the seashore; and your descendants shall possess the gate of their enemies."

Abraham was strong in faith because he kept his focus, his mind, on the promise of God. Every time he looked at the stars, he was reminded of the promise. And every time he looked at the sand, he was reminded of the promise. Hope kept him on course until faith created the substance in his and Sarah's life, a baby boy!

The Christian's One and Only Problem

All your achievements and your failures are the result of your thinking. Christians have one problem: their carnal thinking.

> For those who live according to the flesh set their minds on the things of the flesh, but those who live according to the Spirit, the things of the Spirit. For to be carnally minded is death, but to be spiritually minded is life and peace. Because the carnal mind is enmity against God; for it is not subject to the law of God, nor indeed can be. So then, those who are in the flesh cannot please God.
>
> Romans 8:5–8

Remember what Proverbs 4:23 says, "Keep your heart with all diligence, for out of it spring the issues of life."

If you find out that your problem is not your faith but your thinking, you should put all your effort into renewing your mind to the will of God. You should focus on training and developing your thought life to *benefit* you instead of allowing it to be a detriment to your life. Develop it to produce good things in your life so you can glorify God.

We fight with thoughts—spiritual thoughts versus carnal thoughts. If you're not prepared for a battle, you will most definitely lose. You see, if you don't prepare to win, you have prepared to lose, which is exactly what will happen. As I said earlier, the battle is either won or lost in your mind. Therefore, we must continually prepare our minds for action if we want to win the war against the carnal thoughts that produces death in our lives.

The Bible says that we should be "casting down imaginations, and every high thing that exalteth itself against the knowledge of God, and bringing into captivity every thought to the obedience of Christ" (2 Cor. 10:5 KJV).

You might be thinking: We have thousands of thoughts during the course of the day, and God is asking us to capture every thought we have and make it obedient to Jesus' will for our lives. But you don't have a clue how to do that! Rest assured that if God told us to do something, He has already provided us the ability to do it, with His help. You just have to believe it. You must guard your thoughts, which means to check each thought that comes to your mind. If the thought is not God's will for your life, or if it is a carnal thought that carries death with it, then cast it down and replace it with the Word of God, which produces life.

This might sound like a lot to do, but it is an ongoing practice. In other words, you have to be diligent enough to make this a lifestyle in order to build the good treasure in your heart that will produce good things.

God tells us to cast down "imaginations and every high thing" that exalts itself against His will for our lives. And we are to embrace His will and thoughts because whoever controls your thoughts or imagination will control your belief system and will, therefore, control your life. Your belief system is comprised of the words you hear, thoughts you dwell on, and the pictures that fill your imagination. Your imagination (what you believe) and faith must work together, if you want to enjoy the promises of the kingdom.

The mistake most Christians make is that they think believing and faith are synonymous. But they are not. *Faith* is a noun and *believe* is an action verb.

We already established that if you are born again, you have the faith of Jesus. But is that faith enough to receive the promises? Hebrews 6:12 says that "through faith and patience [we] inherit the promises." Anytime you exercise faith, there is always an element of patience involved. Patience is what keeps faith on the job long enough to deliver you your desire.

In Lystra a certain man without strength in his feet was sitting, a cripple from his mother's womb, who had never walked. This man heard Paul speaking. Paul, observing him intently and seeing that he had faith to be healed, said with a loud voice, 'Stand up straight on your feet!' And he leaped and walked.

Acts 14:8–10

I want you to notice that this man in Acts 14 had faith to be healed, yet he was still on the ground, still a cripple—until he acted on that faith. You see, believing is acting on your faith. Without action, faith is dead. or it is non-productive. The law of faith is always available, but it is dormant until someone makes a demand on that law with his or her actions.

Faith and Believing

Acting on what you believe releases the creative power of faith.

Therefore, I say to you, whatever things you ask when you pray, believe that you receive them, and you will have them.

Mark 11:24

Praying "in faith" without acting like your prayers have been answered is not faith. It is doubt. It's unbelief. Faith can only express itself or its creative power through the actions of your belief. You will only receive what you believe you receive because what you truly believe will always foster actions, and those actions will put a demand on faith to create that thing in your life.

Jesus said to him, "If you can believe, all things are possible to him who believes."

Mark 9:23

You were created to believe. Every day, you are believing for things. And you are receiving things, whether good things or bad. What you believe is what is causing your successes or failures.

What you believe is what fills your heart and your thoughts. What you focus on becomes your imagination, a cluster of thoughts that you dwell on. When you dwell on them daily, they produce negative or positive pictures in your heart, which, in turn, foster words and actions that frame your future.

Your life is a reflection of all your habitual thoughts and imaginations.

A good man out of the good treasure of his heart brings forth good things, and an evil man out of the evil treasure brings forth evil things.

Matthew 12:35

Thoughts are the building blocks of your future, so be careful—be mindful—of the blocks you use. What you are seeing in your heart and mind will determine what your faith will create in your life.

The "treasures" of your heart, or your imaginations, are what make up your belief system. And nothing is impossible to those who believe. What you believe is all that faith has to work to create good in your life.

Jesus said, "According to your faith be it unto you" (Matt. 9:29 KJV). Whatever is "being unto you" is because that is all that you've given faith to work with. Good things or evil things—they all come from what you believe.

Remember, you only receive what you believe you receive, according to the law of faith (see Rom. 3:27). Now, you see how important it is to practice and train yourself to "cast... down imaginations, and every high thing that exalteth itself against the knowledge of God, and bringing into captivity every thought to the obedience of Christ" (2 Cor. 10:5 KJV).

As you make the instructions in this book a lifestyle, you will experience God's will that "you may prosper in all things and be in health, just as your soul prospers" (3 John v. 2).

www.ingramcontent.com/pod-product-compliance
Lightning Source LLC
Chambersburg PA
CBHW031927090426
42811CB00002B/111